**DO NOT REMOVE
CARDS FROM POCKET**

1980 U.S.
HOCKEY TEAM

by
Wayne Coffey

BLACKBIRCH PRESS, INC.
Woodbridge, Connecticut

Published by Blackbirch Press, Inc.
One Bradley Road
Woodbridge, CT 06525

©1993 Blackbirch Press, Inc.
First Edition

Manufactured in the United States of America

10 9 8 7 6 5 4 3 2 1

Editor: Bruce Glassman
Photo Research: Grace How
Illustrations: Dick Smolinski

Library of Congress Cataloging-in-Publication Data

Coffey, Wayne R.
 1980 U.S. Hockey Team / Wayne Coffey. — 1st ed.
  p.   cm. — (Olympic gold!)
 Includes bibliographical references and index.
 Summary: Recalls events at the 1980 Winter Olympics where the young, talented United States hockey team stunned the world by winning a gold medal.
 ISBN 1-56711-007-X
 1.Hockey—United States—Juvenile Literature.
2. Winter Olympic Games (13th: 1980: Lake Placid, New York)—Juvenile literature. [1. Hockey—History. 2. Winter Olympic Games (13th: 1980: Lake Placid, New York).]
I. Title. II. Title: 1980 US hockey team. III. Title: 1980 United States hockey team. IV. Series.
GV48.4.U6C64 1993
796.962 '0973—dc20   92-21231
                                           CIP
                                           AC

Contents

1

Before the Games

"When we're good, we're very, very good, and when we're bad, we're horrid."

As the 1980 Winter Olympics began in Lake Placid, New York, the United States was going through a difficult time. Americans were being held hostage by Iran, a crisis that lasted for 444 days. Then, after Soviet troops stormed into Afghanistan, people worried that U.S. troops might be sent in to try to head them off. At home, inflation was rising. Family budgets everywhere were feeling the pinch.

These events left the nation with a sense of helplessness. People were angry about the hostages and frustrated because they couldn't do anything about it. President Jimmy Carter and millions of Americans

Opposite:
Team USA members embrace William Baker after he scored the tying goal in their first Olympic match. Baker's goal enabled the team to continue on in the competition.

5

looked to the Olympics in Lake Placid, a village in northern New York State, for a little relief. If ever there were a need for something to root for, this was it.

Winter Olympic sports are not usually strong events for the United States. Outside of figure skating and speed skating, the United States has often had a difficult time keeping up with the cold-weather countries of Europe. After all, athletes from nations such as Austria, Germany, Sweden, Finland, and Switzerland have had centuries of experience skiing, skating, and bobsledding.

The difference in skill between Europe and the United States was also clear in ice hockey, which had been dominated by the Soviets since 1956. So powerful were the Soviet hockey players that most experts thought of them as the best team in the entire world—even better than the leading clubs in the National Hockey League (NHL). In fact, the Soviets had recently beaten a team of NHL All-Stars. The team won six straight games in a series of contests against the best talent the league had to offer.

The only time since 1956 that the Soviets had failed to capture the Olympic gold was in 1960. The Games that winter were held in the United States, in mountainous Squaw Valley, California. The U.S. hockey team pulled off a surprise string of upsets, defeating the Canadians, the Soviets, and the Czechs for the gold.

The 1960 U.S. squad came to be known as the "Team of Destiny." It accomplished one of the most remarkable feats in U.S. Olympic history. But there was no reason to believe that the 1980 team was capable of repeating the earlier victories. The average age of the U.S. players was 22 years old, making them the youngest hockey team ever to play in the Games. The Americans had some talented players, but not nearly as many as other countries had. When the 12 countries competing in ice hockey were ranked before competition, the United States placed seventh—behind the USSR, Czechoslovakia, Sweden, Canada, Finland, and West Germany.

A Pre-Olympic Setback

Before heading to Lake Placid, the U.S. team wrapped up its long training period with an exhibition game against the mighty Soviets at Madison Square Garden in New York City. This was the final test for the young Americans—and they flunked it. The Soviets trounced them, 10-3. The visitors skated so fluidly that there were times when it looked as if the Americans were glued to the ice. The Soviet team

kept hitting shots at the American goal, leading by 4-0 at the end of just one period. The American crowd experienced very few moments worth cheering at.

It seemed to be a terrible note to start the Olympics on. And yet Herb Brooks, the coach, didn't appear to be at all concerned. At least he wasn't showing any concern outwardly. "Sometimes a good kicking is good for a quality team and for quality athletes," the coach said. "We won't be demoralized."

Herb Brooks was considered a masterful hockey coach. At the time, he was coach of the University of Minnesota team and was almost an Olympian himself once. Back in 1960, young Herb was the final player cut from that future Team of Destiny.

After losing a pre-Olympic exhibition game to the Soviets, U.S. coach Brooks said, "Sometimes a good kicking is good for a quality team and for quality athletes."

Now, in 1980, Brooks needed to have every member of his young group play hard and smart. He stressed an attacking style that featured speedy skating and sharp passing. Such a style puts a lot of pressure on the players to keep the puck under control. It also makes the slightest lapse in concentration a possible big mistake. The defeat by the Soviets at Madison Square Garden might have given his team just the boost in concentration it needed, Brooks thought.

9

But Herb Brooks wasn't looking for any sort of miracle in Lake Placid. He knew how tough the Soviets were. When someone asked what the United States's chances were of winning the gold medal, the coach said, "Slim and none."

Regardless of the odds, 19 of America's best hockey talents would travel to upstate New York to do their best for their country. The team members were: James Craig, Kenneth Morrow, Michael Ramsey, William Baker, John O'Callahan, Bob Suter, David Silk, Neal Broten, Mark Johnson, Steven Christoff, Mark Wells, Mark Pavelich, Eric Strobel, Michael Eruzione (captain), David Christian, Robert McClanahan, William "Buzz" Schneider, Philip Verchota, and John Harrington.

Brooks liked his team, but consistency on the ice was a problem. The coach wasn't sure what he would get from the players. "When we're good, we're very, very good," he said. "And when we're bad, we're horrid." The coach believed that if his team was very good in Lake Placid, it might sneak away with a bronze medal. As Team USA awaited its opening game against a superb Swedish club, the skaters were unaware that they were about to start one of the greatest experiences of their lives.

2

Gaining Momentum and Fans

Hockey fever suddenly overtook the village.

The way hockey competition is set up in the Olympics, every game takes on tremendous importance. The 12 teams are divided into two, 6-team divisions. Each team plays the other 5 teams in its division. Back in 1980, only the top 2 teams in each division were advanced to the medal round. Everybody else went home.

Team USA, as the American squad was called, had little margin for error. With such powerful teams as Czechoslovakia and Sweden in the same division, an early defeat could mean a quick end to any hopes for a U.S. medal.

Taking on the Swedes

The first opponent for the United States was Sweden. The swift-skating Swedes liked to joke that their Olympic players were merely their "B" team. Their "A" team was busy playing in the National Hockey League. But this was a better-than-average B team— a highly skilled group with a young goaltender named Per-Eric "Pelle" Lindbergh. Then just 20 years old, Lindbergh would go on to become an NHL All-Star for the Philadelphia Flyers. But for millions of youngsters, he would also become a tragic symbol of the dangers of drinking and driving. At the peak of his NHL career, Pelle died in a drunken-driving accident.

Coach Brooks knew he had to take a gamble against the Swedes.

In the game against the United States, the Swedes took an early 1-0 lead. After Team USA tied the score, Thomas Eriksson of Sweden whistled a shot past U.S. goaltender Jim Craig. It gave the Swedes a 2-1 lead in the third (final) period.

The Americans were having no success in getting through Swedish defense. Time was growing short. Coach Brooks knew he had to take a gamble for his team to make the tying goal. As the game entered its final minute, Jim Craig raced to the U.S. bench. He was replaced on the ice by an extra skater. This way, the Americans had six skating players on the attack against the five Swedish skaters. Leaving the goal without a goaltender was a great risk, of course. All the Swedes had to do was get control of the puck, and they had a good chance of scoring an easy goal and taking the game.

At that point, team USA controlled the puck and hurried forward into Sweden's end. The American skaters spread themselves out to take advantage of their extra man. Even the smallest mishandling of the slippery puck would probably mean defeat.

The puck skidded toward the point where Bill Baker, captain of the University of Minnesota team, controlled it. Only 27 seconds remained. Baker saw an opening. He whipped his stick back and rocketed a slap shot from 55 feet out. Lindbergh did his best to block it, but he couldn't get to the puck in time. Baker's blast zoomed by him and into the net.

Teammates mobbed Baker. The Swedes looked dazed; their lead had slipped away in the final half-minute.

The American bench exploded. Teammates mobbed Baker. The Swedes looked stunned; their lead had slipped away in the final half-minute. The contest ended with a 2-2 tie, but Team USA was certainly much happier with the tie than the Swedes were. The Americans knew that they had escaped by the narrowest of margins.

Trying to Cancel the Czechs

The next challenge for Team USA was a big one indeed—Czechoslovakia. In their first game, the Czechs trounced Norway, 11-0. While most observers in Lake Placid were surprised that the youthful Americans tied Sweden, they knew that the awesome Czech team was another story. The Czechs were favored to meet the Soviet Union in the finals. And when Czechoslovakia scored just two minutes into the match, it looked as if it might be a crushing defeat.

But the United States was not finished surprising people. Mike Eruzione, the team captain and the college roommate of goalie

With 27 seconds left on the clock, Bill Baker fired a shot from 55 feet out to tie the match and keep the U.S. team in the running for a gold medal.

Jim Craig, powered a drive from the left side to tie the score at 1-1. Then Mark Pavelich gave the United States a 2-1 lead when he beat Czech goalie, Jiri Kralik, from in close.

Before the fast-paced first period was over, the Czechs had tied the score again. Marian Stastny, a right wing, scored on a pass from his center, brother Peter Stastny. Still another Stastny, Anton, was the left wing on the line. Like the rest of their teammates, the Stastny brothers were not expecting to get locked in a close game with the Americans.

The truth is, the game wasn't close much longer. The U.S. team seemed to get a boost in that first period. Coach Brooks had warned the skaters not to be in awe of any team. He pushed them constantly to make certain every player was giving maximum effort at all times.

With the pro-American crowd roaring its support, Team USA thoroughly outplayed the Czechs the rest of the way. Brooks changed players frequently, and the success of using fresh legs showed. American skaters buzzed from one end of the ice to the other. They seemed to collect every loose puck, doing all they could to keep Czechoslovakia in trouble. The United States did not let up.

15

"We wanted to win so badly," the U.S. forward Mike Ramsey said. "The feeling in the locker room was unbelievable. It's an emotional high. To think you can stay that high for sixty minutes is unbelievable."

But Team USA did exactly that. Buzz Schneider tallied two goals. Mark Johnson, the team's most aggressive scorer, added another. By the time the game was over, the United States was a 7-3 winner.

Hockey Fever

Word spread rapidly through Lake Placid's frosty winter air. People could hardly believe it. "Did the Americans really beat the Czechs?" people asked in amazement.

Hockey fever suddenly overtook the village. U.S. hockey fans began waving miniature American flags everywhere they went. Throughout the country, newspapers were filled with stories about the excitement that surrounded the team. The crowds became so big that the field house looked as if it might burst. There were dozens of other Olympic events going on. But not even the speed-skating heroics of Eric Heiden, who would win five gold medals at those Games, could overshadow what was going on in the hockey rink.

Word spread rapidly through Lake Placid's frosty winter air. People could hardly believe it. "Did the Americans really beat the Czechs?" people asked in amazement.

Hockey fever gripped America after the U.S. team defeated the Czechs in the second match of the Olympics.

After such an emotional victory, Brooks was concerned that his players might suffer a letdown in the next game, which was against Norway. A stern, hard-driving man, Brooks made it plain to his players that this was no time to let up.

The players heeded their coach's warning, emerging with a strong 5-1 victory over the Norwegians. Team USA followed the Norway game with its finest effort yet, a 7-2 victory over Romania. The Americans unleashed an amazing 51 shots at the Romanian goal. They skated fast, worked hard, and got terrific play from Craig. Teamwork and unselfishness became the U.S. hallmarks.

Next, with a 4-2 triumph over the West Germans, Team USA clinched a spot in the medal round, along with the Soviet Union, Sweden, and Finland. The U.S. team had already accomplished much more than most people expected. From here, it was going to get lots harder. Only the most fearsome teams remained. The Americans, for all they had done, still had no guarantee of even a bronze medal. And now their joyride was taking them up against the greatest hockey team in the world, the Soviet Union.

Even though both the United States and Sweden had identical records of 3-0-1, and even though they had played to a 2-2 tie, the Swedes were ranked first in the division because of Sweden's advantage in goals scored and goals allowed. By drawing the top ranking, Sweden was spared having to play the Soviets in the semifinal round. Instead, the Swedish team was paired against its Scandinavian neighbors, the Finns.

The Americans were about to square off against a team that had destroyed them, with a score of 10-3, not even two weeks earlier. U.S. hockey fans, Coach Brooks, and his team, were hoping that somehow *that* piece of history would not repeat itself in Lake Placid.

3

Facing a "Mountain"

"We can't make a mistake all night."

t was hard for the youthful Americans not to be in awe of the Soviet hockey players. There was a special mystery about them. They were, after all, the finest collection of hockey players in the world.

From 1956 through 1988, the USSR earned a record of 53-5-1 in Olympic competition. It won seven gold medals and outscored opponents by an unheard-of total: 411 to 111 total goals. Although the first organized game of ice hockey was played in Canada in the mid-1800s, the Soviets did not start playing it seriously until almost one hundred years later. But they certainly made up for lost time!

Preparing for the Challenge

The Soviets were so tough that people weren't kidding when they said that their hardest games were played when they had to face one another in practice. It was impossible not to come away impressed by the skillful puck movement, speedy skating, and blistering shots. The Soviet goalie was a towering man named Vladislav Tretiak, who was often hailed as the finest puck-stopper in the world. The team captain was a 35-year-old center, Boris Mikhailov, who was another supreme talent. Defenseman Valery Vasilyev was a hard, accurate shooter who rarely made mistakes.

Determined and dedicated as the American players were, very few of them, if any, would have even been able to make the Soviet team. Coach Brooks did not want his players to forget the huge difference in pure hockey skill. Over and over, the coach would say, "We don't have the talent to win games here. We have to do it on talent, work, cohesion, and rhythm." The coach wasn't looking to embarrass his players. He simply wanted to emphasize that a total team effort was required to even make a game of it with the Soviets.

Opposite:
Vladislav Tretiak, the goalie for the Soviet team, was a towering man considered by many the best defender in the game.

The Soviets were so tough that people weren't kidding when they said that their hardest games were when they had to face one another in practice.

21

The Americans had just one day to prepare for the Soviets after the U.S. victory over West Germany. The game was to be played at 5 P.M. on Friday afternoon. The date was February 22. As the moment approached, it was clear that, while dozens of events were going on all over town, the one event that mattered most was about to begin in the Olympic field house.

Standing Room Only

The arena was packed to the rafters with 10,000 fans. When the seats were filled, people kept piling in to watch standing up. Tickets cost up to $67, but by game time those little pieces of cardboard were more valuable than gold.

The fans were in a frenzy even before the puck was dropped that Friday evening. U.S. flags waved in all corners of the rink. People bellowed the now-familiar chant: "USA, USA." The atmosphere was electric, as if this were the Super Bowl and the seventh game of the World Series rolled into one. Millions of Americans had hoped that the Olympics would give them something to forget the nation's troubles. And when all was done, they got something very special.

"We can't make a mistake all night," said Craig Patrick, the assistant coach to Herb

Brooks. "This is for all the money—well, not money, all the glory."

In preparing for the game, the coaches reminded the team that it could not afford to draw penalties against the Soviets. In hockey, a penalized player must leave the ice, usually for two minutes. When the Soviets had a man advantage, they were just about unstoppable.

The players got last-minute instructions. Nobody needed to tell them that they had to play the game of their lives.

One thing was noticeably different from previous games. Herb Brooks was almost always stern, but now the coach wasn't scowling or warning his players the way he usually did. He wanted them to give their maximum effort. But he also wanted them to appreciate the moment. On a yellow pad Coach Brooks scrawled out a few words. Minutes before the players left the locker room to play the USSR, the coach showed them what he had written. The pad said, "You were born to be a player. You were meant to be here."

Minutes before Team USA went to play the Soviets, Coach Brooks showed his players what he had written on a pad. It said, "You were born to be a player. You were meant to be here."

Team USA stormed out toward the ice, full of fire and enthusiasm. The players couldn't have been any higher if they were standing on a mountaintop. Now they had a mountain of a team to try to overcome.

23

4

Toppling the "Mountain"

"Do you believe in miracles?"

From the moment they took the ice in their bright red uniforms, the Soviets could sense the electricity filling the air in the Olympic field house. It was as if the charge of the crowd were flowing right into Team USA. Whatever the American skaters were lacking in talent, they were more than making up for in grit.

The players had barely broken a sweat, when Soviet star, Valery Kharlamov, was slammed by a couple of eager Americans. It was a good, hard, legal check. The jolt lifted Kharlamov right off the ice, and it was a clear sign that the Americans were not thinking about the Soviets' reputation.

Opposite:
Only a few minutes into the game, Soviet star Valery Kharlamov (number 14) was taken out by an incredible slam from the determined Americans.

Back in the goal, Jim Craig was totally focused on the action in front of him. The goalie knew it was critical to be at his best, especially early in the game. It would give his teammates a big morale boost if Craig could turn aside the hard-driving Soviet shots. It would make them want to push themselves even harder.

About nine minutes into the first period, Aleksei Kasatonov ripped a slap shot toward the U.S. goal. Craig was poised to stop it when, in front of the net, Vladimir Krutov deflected the puck. The puck changed its course and slipped by Craig. There was nothing more Craig could have done. The noise in the field house ceased. The Soviets had a 1-0 lead.

The Americans couldn't afford to get too far behind against the Soviets. If they did, they would have to gamble on the attack. This would leave openings for the Soviets to take advantage of. They kept skating hard, passing beautifully, trying to create opportunities. With six minutes left in the first period, they got one. Buzz Schneider, 24, was the oldest player on the team. He fired a shot toward the upper-right-hand corner. Tretiak, the Soviet goalie, couldn't catch up to it. The arena exploded with deafening cheers as Schneider's shot tied the score, 1-1.

Beating the Clock

The Soviets quickly answered with another goal, and it appeared that they would take the 2-1 lead into the intermission. But in the closing seconds of the period, U.S. defenseman Ken Morrow smacked a desperation shot from center ice. The puck bounced out toward the front of the goal. A couple of players got their sticks on it, and then Mark Johnson scooped it up and drove it past a stunned Tretiak. The puck *The puck went in at almost exactly the same time the clock showed 0:00.* went in at almost exactly the same time the clock showed 0:00. The Soviets argued that it was too late, and it shouldn't count. The Americans held their breath. After a conference among the officials, the ruling was that Johnson's goal was good, making the score 2-2. It was a shocking conclusion to the period, and another shock followed soon after. The Soviet coaches chose to replace Tretiak with Vladimir Myshkin, a good player, but not nearly in the class of Tretiak. Later, a Soviet assistant coach would say of Tretiak, "He is not playing well, and my feeling is he was nervous."

The gripping contest stayed close the rest of the way. There was nonstop action. Bodies crunched into one another. Players battled hard for every loose puck. Using the best Soviet strategies, the Americans

27

passed crisply, weaving in and out. They played well, but the Soviet defense proved tough to crack. The Americans had just two shots on goal in the second period. Meanwhile, taking advantage of a U.S. penalty, the USSR got a goal from Aleksandr Maltsev to regain the lead, 3-2.

With just one period to go, the U.S. players were heartened by where they stood. They were in a one-goal game with the finest hockey team in the world. They weren't backing down. With a crowd of 10,000 roaring, flag-waving supporters, how could they?

Tension and excitement mounted with each passing minute as the final period got under way. Each and every possession was critical. Every mistake could turn into disaster. Pressing the attack, American Dave Silk carried the puck into the Soviet zone. He collided with a Soviet defenseman, but the puck squirted free. Mark Johnson alertly got control of it, about six feet in front of Myshkin. Johnson pulled back his stick and snapped off a shot. Goal!

Just about 11 1/2 minutes remained in the dead-locked drama. The United States had come this far. But could Team USA finish the job?

Mark Johnson, a buddy of speed-skating marvel Eric Heiden at the University of Wisconsin, had tied the game. The field house sounded like a spaceship at blast-off.

Johnson's excited red-white-and-blue-clad teammates mobbed him, rubbing his head. Team USA had a fresh start.

Just about 11 1/2 minutes remained in the deadlocked drama. On the ice, all over the arena, hearts pounded with anticipation. The United States had come this far. The players had far surpassed all expectations. But could Team USA finish the job?

Getting a Lead

Just 80 seconds after Johnson's tying goal, team captain Mike Eruzione bolted off the bench on a line change, replacing Buzz Schneider. Eruzione's linemates, Mark Pavelich and John Harrington, pushed the attack. When the puck slithered loose, Eruzione controlled it and skated toward the middle of the ice, between the face-off circles. He was about 30 feet out. With a defender in front of him, Eruzione saw an opening. He anchored himself and then drilled the puck toward the goal. The next instant, the puck was behind Myshkin, in the net, and the arena was exploding once more. Myshkin, blocked by his defender, never got a good view of the shot. He got a piece of it, but not enough. Now it was Eruzione's turn to be mobbed. Overjoyed, he did a crazy, high-stepping dance and was engulfed by his teammates.

Eruzione's goal gave the United States its first lead of the game, 4-3. Exactly 10 minutes remained. It seemed like an eternity against the dangerous Soviets. The roar of the crowd never stopped the rest of the way. It felt as if the pure excitement were going to blow the roof off the building.

After the team tied the game against the USSR, Mike Eruzione saw an opening from about 30 feet out. He drilled the puck past the Soviet goalie and did a high-stepping dance of triumph when the goal scored.

The Soviets attacked the U.S. goal with newly found determination. They skated hard, passed fluidly, and whacked shots at Craig. But the goaltender turned aside one great shot after another. As the seconds ticked away, the Soviets, in desperation,

began dumping the puck into the American end, hoping for a good bounce or a mistake by a U.S. defenseman. The Soviets would often use their superior puck-control skills and attack with sharp passes. But it seemed now as if they were panicking.

In the final minute, the Soviets did all they could to mount a rush toward the U.S. goal. But throughout the dramatic final minutes, the Americans were playing with poise and precision. They weren't coughing up the puck or giving the Soviets the big chance they needed.

In the final minute, the Soviets did all they could to mount a rush toward the U.S. goal.

The wild crowd was counting down the final seconds: "Ten . . . nine . . . eight . . . ." Team USA kept skating, concentrating. ". . . three . . . two . . . one . . . ." The horn sounded, the spectators roared, and all the previous celebrations seemed mild by comparison. The whole team poured onto the ice. Everybody piled in a happy heap on top of Jim Craig. The excited fans waved flags and started one more "USA" chant. The players hugged. Some of them cried. Others looked too stunned to do anything but ask themselves, "Did this really happen?" Coach Brooks, overcome with emotion, locked himself in a men's room for a while. It gave him a chance to savor what had just happened.

After the Win

As the Americans celebrated their victory, the Soviet players stood almost statuelike at the far end of the ice. Many of them looked dazed, like worn-out punch-drunk prizefighters. A few smiled at the joyful outpouring before them.

In the locker room, the players began singing "God Bless America," but they were so excited that not everybody could remember the words. Mark Johnson later told reporters, "We only had two shots on net in the second period, but we were only losing three to two, and that's when we knew we had a chance to win. . . . Being behind by only one goal, we knew we were younger, we knew we could outskate them, and we knew we were going to break our butts to beat them. And we did."

They did, indeed. The celebration raged over Lake Placid almost the entire night. People danced and sang in the streets. Fireworks exploded in the dark sky. On television, broadcaster Al Michaels ended the game by saying, "Do you believe in miracles?" In Lake Placid, and all over the country, the answer was a strong yes. It turned out that Coach Brooks had been right when he scribbled that message to his team on the yellow pad before the game. This was their moment.

(Continued on page 49)

1980

LAKE PLACID, UNITED STATES

THE GAMES BEGIN

The rolling hills of Lake Placid, New York, created a dramatic backdrop for the opening ceremonies of the XIII Winter Olympiad in 1980.

A LAST-MINUTE SAVE

The Swedes took an early lead in the first Olympic hockey competition. Soon after the Americans tied the score at 1-1, Thomas Eriksson of Sweden fired a shot past goalie Jim Craig to put the Swedes ahead in the third and final period. With 27 seconds remaining on the clock, American Bill Baker saw an opening. From 55 feet out, Baker rocketed a slap shot past the goaltender and into the net to tie the score and save the day. *Below*: Mark Wells (number 6) guards teammate Bill Baker (number 15) as they move down the ice against Sweden. Baker scored the final goal for the American team in that game. *Opposite*: Team USA coach Herb Brooks watches nervously as his team battles Sweden on the Olympic ice.

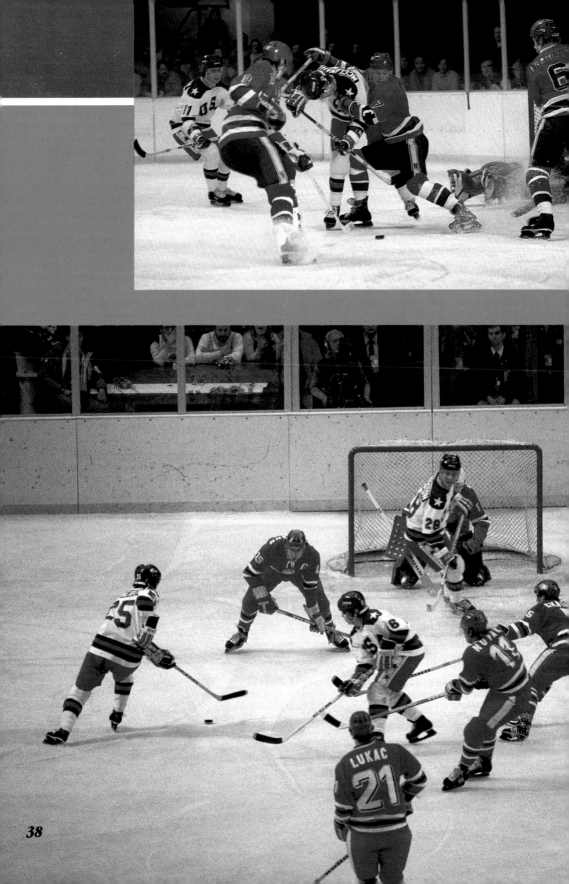

ON A ROLL

Hockey fever swept through Lake Placid after the Americans beat the highly respected Czechoslovakian team with a score of 7-3. Miniature American flags could be seen waving in drugstores and gas stations all across the country. By the time game number three against Norway came around, Coach Brooks urged his players to keep their focus and concentration up. The Norwegians, he warned, were a skillful team. The players listened to their coach and went on to beat Norway soundly with a 5-1 victory. *Below:* Eric Strobel battles for control of the puck. *Opposite bottom:* William "Buzz" Schneider (number 25) sets up for a pass to waiting teammate John Harrington (number 16). *Opposite top:* Rob McClanahan's attempt at a goal is checked by a Norwegian player.

TEAMWORK WINS THE DAY

Team USA followed their victory against Norway with their finest effort yet, a 7-2 win over Romania. In total, the Americans fired an incredible 51 shots at the Romanian goal, displaying a new level of skill and tough determination on the ice. Their next game, against West Germany, ended in an impressive 4-2 triumph. With the West German win, the U.S. team had clinched a spot in the medal round. *Below and opposite:* U.S. captain Mike Eruzione in action as he sets up for a shot on the Romanian goal and then waits for a pass before he scores.

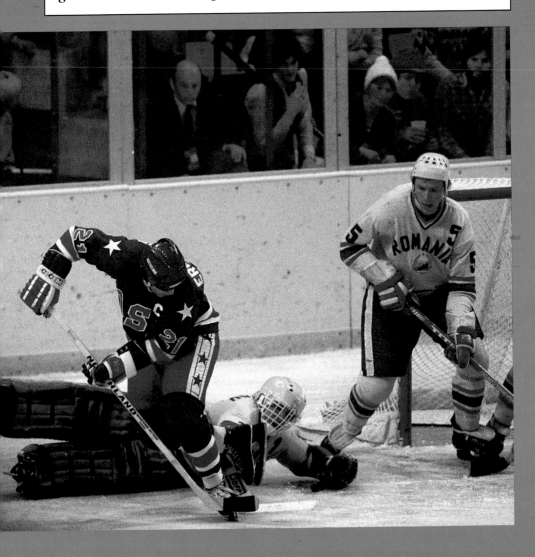

Taking on Hockey's Giants

Before 1980, the Soviet team had dominated the international ice-hockey scene for decades. Though the Americans had played incredibly up to this point, many people doubted that they could actually pull out a win against the finest hockey team in the world. In the closing seconds of the first period, the Americans were behind 2-1. In a desperation shot from center ice, Ken Morrow smacked the puck toward the goal, where teammate Mark Johnson scooped it up and scored just as the clock showed 0:00. Though there was controversy over whether to count it, the officials ruled in favor of the Americans, making the score 2-2. In the next period, Mark Johnson saved the day again, scoring another goal to tie the score. Little more than a minute later, team captain Mike Eruzione slammed a goal from about 30 feet out to give his team their first lead of the match. In the final minutes, the USSR pressed hard but could not come up with a goal. When the final buzzer sounded, Team USA had beaten the Soviets. *Below*: Buzz Schneider shoots a goal into the net to tie the match at 1-1. *Opposite top:* Mark Johnson fights for control before scoring one of his two tying goals. *Opposite bottom:* Members of Team USA watch anxiously as the action unfolds during the match against the USSR.

UNEXPECTED TRIUMPH

The Olympic crowd went wild when the clock ran out on the USSR, putting the U.S. team into the gold-medal round against Finland. Here, Team USA huddles together in a victory celebration. *Below:* The Soviet team looks on as their gold-medal chances slip away in the final minutes of the game.

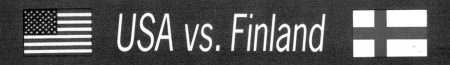
THE GOLD-MEDAL GAME

Things did not look good for the Americans as they skated out for the third period of their final match. They were down 2-1 and their attack on the Finns was not working. If they were going to take the lead, they had to play more aggressively and take some chances. Two minutes into the final period, Dave Christian saw an opening, swooped into Finn territory, and slid the puck to teammate Phil Verchota, who fired a goal from 15 feet out. A huge roar filled the stadium. The American team had tied the game. Here, Phil Verchota approaches the puck before scoring.

THE MIRACLE COMES TRUE

After Phil Verchota tied the game, the Americans needed to keep the pressure on. Four minutes later, Mark Johnson passed the puck to Rob McClanahan, who rocketed a shot past the Finn goalie. Team USA was in the lead for the first time in the match. As the clock wound down, Finland could not penetrate the American defense. With just a few minutes left in the game, Mark Johnson sealed Finland's fate by rushing the goal and rifling a shot into the net to give the United States a 4-2 lead. It was a lead the Finns could not overcome. *Right*: Mark Johnson raises his arms in triumph after scoring the final goal for his team. *Above*: America's gold-medal hockey team explodes in celebration as the clock runs out.

GOLD FOR THE UNDERDOGS

Nobody, including Coach Brooks, ever dreamed that the American team could go as far as they did in the 1980 Games. But each game that they played showed more and more what determination, discipline, and cooperation can accomplish for a team that has the drive to be the very best. Here, the newly crowned Olympic champions acknowledge the crowd as they huddle in celebration on top of the awards platform.

(Continued from page 32)

5

From Challenge to Victory

*"You're watching a group of people who startled
the athletic world."*

There was just one complication for the U.S. hockey team after the stunning upset of the Soviet Union. The American skaters still had one even more important hockey game to play!

The victory on Friday night, February 22, was so emotional that it felt as though the United States had won the gold medal. But that wasn't the case. Team USA had to take on Finland two days later, on Sunday morning. Only a victory over the Finns would toss the Olympic gold medal to the Americans. Under the Olympic scoring system, if the Americans were to lose, the gold would go to the Soviets.

Goaltender Jim Craig said, "If we don't win against Finland, people will forget about the triumph over the Soviets."

This in itself presented a stiff challenge to the Americans. Because they were very young and had already achieved so much more than expected, it would be easy for them to suffer a letdown. Coach Herb Brooks

Even after its stunning upset over the Soviets, the U.S. team still had one more game to play.

knew that, after Friday night's victory, it would not be easy to get his skaters thoroughly focused and ready to play on Sunday. Another problem was that now there was pressure on the United States to win. Team USA had something very big to lose. Up until this point, everything the Americans had accomplished was a bonus, since nobody figured they would be in the running for the medal anyway.

The coach did everything he could to bring the players back to earth. He stressed his usual themes—nonstop hard work and total unselfishness. He warned them that they weren't talented enough to be over-confident. The players listened, but they were fresh off the greatest thrill of their lives. It was going to be tough to play with as much emotion against Finland.

The concerns turned out to be well placed. It was clear from the outset that the U.S. players did not have quite the same fire they had on Friday night. Although the Olympic field house was filled with 10,000 fans, the Sunday morning crowd wasn't as pumped as the throng on Friday night.

The Finns, a solid, defensive-minded team with very good stick-handlers, were not to be taken lightly. Finland scored the game's first goal midway through the first period. After the second period, the Finns continued to lead, 2-1, despite a goal by Steve Christoff of Team USA.

Now only one period remained. If the Americans were going to get their gold, they were going to have to come from behind—as they had done in five of their six previous games. It wasn't going to be easy. The U.S. attack was not clicking. The passes were not penetrating the Finn defense. Jim Craig had permitted only two goals, but he did not look as sharp as he had throughout the tournament.

Only one period remained. If the Americans were going to get their gold, they were going to have to come from behind.

As the final 20 minutes opened, the Americans pulled together. They were determined to put more pressure on the Finns. Just more than 2 minutes into the period, the U.S. team broke free on a two-against-one rush. Racing toward the goal with the puck was Dave Christian, whose father, Billy, was an Olympic hero of 1960. That year, in the third period of a

game against another powerful Soviet club, Billy Christian scored two goals to spark the United States to a 3-2 victory. Both goals were assisted by Roger Christian, who was Billy's brother and Dave's uncle. Dave was just a baby at the time.

A Score to Tie

As Dave Christian swooped into the Finns' end, he spotted linemate Phil Verchota free on the left side. Christian slid him a pass, and Verchota fired a shot from 15 feet out, beating Finland goalie, Jorma Valtonen. A huge cheer exploded through the tense arena crowd. The score was tied at 2-2. Suddenly, the game's momentum had shifted. But would the Americans be able to maintain the attack and get another goal?

Four minutes later, Rob McClanahan provided the answer. Mark Johnson controlled the puck behind the Finn goal, then zipped a pass out front, where McClanahan was stationed, setting himself firmly. As soon as McClanahan received Johnson's pass, he stuffed it past Valtonen. The Americans had the lead for the first time in the contest.

Finland, however, wasn't going to just roll over. After the Americans were penalized, the Finns had a man advantage for two minutes. They passed the puck crisply.

They pinned the U.S. team in its own zone. Four times, they drilled shots at Jim Craig, who was able to steer each of them aside.

Just seconds after the teams were at full strength, the Americans suffered another penalty—Dave Christian was called for tripping. The Finns had another power play, as it's called when a team has the man advantage.

Fewer than 10 minutes remained. In a one-goal-lead game, the pressure was on every player not to have any lapses. When the clock edged under the 5-minute mark, the linesman whistled another penalty. And once again, it was against the Americans. The Finns had another power-play opportunity.

On the U.S. bench, Herb Brooks's face was tense. The players leaned forward, anxiously watching, hoping they could hang on to the slim lead. The field-house crowd tingled from the drama.

When the clock edged under the five-minute mark, the linesman whistled another penalty. And once again, it was against the Americans. The Finns had another power-play opportunity.

Then, with a minute left in the penalty, the U.S. team seized control of the puck. Dave Christian got hold of it and passed it to Mark Johnson, who broke ahead of everybody. The Finns were so intent on pressing the attack that nobody was left back on defense. Johnson had a

53

breakaway. He rushed in on the goaltender and rifled a shot toward the corner. Goal! The United States had scored, in spite of being minus one skater. The Americans now led, 4-2. With just a few minutes to play, Finland could not muster the offense to catch up.

Time Goes—To the Gold

As the seconds ticked away, the celebration began in full force. When the final horn sounded, the rink was a happy madhouse, full of the same scenes as on Friday night: people hugging, crying, and dancing. The victorious players tossed their gloves and sticks up in the air. Relatives and friends skidded onto the ice to share the joy. The fans stood and cheered. They wouldn't stop. It was as if they did not want this moment to ever end. With all the problems in the outside world, people wanted to savor the accomplishments of these 20 college kids.

After being swamped by his teammates, goalie Jim Craig held an American flag in his hands and was searching the crowd, looking for his father. Jim's mother had died not long before. His father had always been very kind and supportive. The heroic goaltender wanted to share the special moment with his dad.

Later, the players tried to explain the powerful emotions that were surging through them.

"There was no way we weren't going to wrap up the gold," Mike Ramsey said.

"I'm sure the twenty guys can't believe it," said Mark Johnson, who scored the final goal for the U.S. team. "They'll probably wake up tomorrow morning and still not believe it."

Among the many fans at the arena was Vice-President Walter Mondale. A native of Minnesota, the vice-president was an avid hockey fan. He stood up, cheering and pumping his fist with each U.S. goal.

"This is one of the greatest moments I've been through in my life," Vice-President Mondale said.

Opposite:
After the clock finally ran out, the U.S. team smothered their goalie, Jim Craig, in jubilation. For days afterward, members of the team could hardly believe that they had actually won it all.

"This is one of the greatest moments I've been through in my life," Vice-President Mondale said.

Shortly after the game, Mr. Mondale's boss, Jimmy Carter, the president of the United States, placed a call to Lake Placid. First the president spoke to Herb Brooks, saying, "We were trying to do business, and nobody could do it. We were watching the TV with one eye and Iran and the economy with the other."

The president expressed his gratitude to team captain Mike Eruzione, who had scored the winning goal against the Soviets two days earlier. "Tell your whole team

Opposite:
Captain Mike Eruzione represented the U.S. team on the victory stand during the ceremony. As the American flag was raised above the others, the Olympic crowd erupted in cheers.

how much I love them, and we look forward to seeing the whole team tomorrow," President Carter said. "They played like true champions. We're so proud of them." The president had invited them to be guests at the White House.

The Moment of Pride

After the Soviet Union trounced Sweden to capture second place later that afternoon, the official ice-hockey medal ceremony was held. Captain Mike Eruzione represented the team on the victory stand. As the American flag was raised toward the rafters, "The Star-Spangled Banner" was played, and it seemed as if the whole arena sang along. When the anthem was over, Eruzione waved to his teammates, and the happy bunch jumped up on the stand. Then they circled the ice and waved to their loyal fans, who had been cheering so hard for them for two weeks. The thrill and excitement would not wear off.

Coach Brooks, who had been the stern taskmaster throughout an entire six months of constant training and competing, was like a proud parent.

"You're watching a group of people who startled the athletic world, not the hockey world, the athletic world," the coach said. "These people are deserving because of

their age and what they had to accomplish in a short time. As a father, you kick your children in the butt a lot, but fathers and mothers love their children, as I love this hockey team."

The jubilation extended beyond Lake Placid. It was a coast-to-coast sensation. There was a nationally televised game between the Kansas City Kings and the Milwaukee Bucks of the National Basketball Association in Kansas City, Missouri. As soon as the victory over Finland was announced, the big crowd stood and sang the national anthem again. In Minnesota, where many of the players hailed from, there were celebrations in living rooms, in restaurants, and in stores. In Winthrop, Massachusetts, Captain Mike Eruzione's hometown, people piled into their cars, and a motorcade took place down the main street. The drivers honked their horns and waved American flags.

"These people are deserving because of their age and what they had to accomplish in a short time," Coach Brooks said.

But maybe the most fitting celebration occurred in the heart of New York City, at the famous Radio City Music Hall. The performance that day was a musical version of "Snow White and the Seven Dwarfs." A little before two o'clock, a young man climbed on stage and told the audience that the United States had won the gold-medal hockey game. The majestic music hall erupted with shouts and exclamations. When the noise subsided, Snow White and the dwarfs came on. The Radio City audience went on to enjoy a delightful fairy tale. But for millions of Americans on Sunday, February 24, 1980, nothing could compare with the fairy tale that came true on the ice in Lake Placid.

Glossary

check A legal body hit allowed in ice hockey.

demoralized Humiliated and embarrassed; disheartened.

exhibition game A contest played as a practice or warm-up, where the outcome does not change a team's official standing in a league.

face-off An attempt by one member of opposing ice-hockey teams to gain first control of the puck when it is dropped at the beginning of a game and after each goal.

goaltender A goalie.

hostages People who are held against their will; usually used as a bargaining chip by terrorists or other criminals.

Olympiad A period of four years from one celebration of the Olympic Games to the next.

power play A situation in ice hockey when one team is temporarily short a player due to a penalty, giving the other team an opportunity to overpower its opponents.

rafters Large supporting beams in the ceiling or roof of a building.

semifinal round The competition before the final round of a championship.

slap shot A shot in ice hockey made with a quick, swinging stroke.

squad In ice hockey, a team of players.

For Further Reading

Aaseng, Nathan. *Great Winter Olympic Moments.* Minneapolis: Lerner Publications, 1990.

Arnold, Caroline. *The Olympic Winter Games.* New York: Franklin Watts, 1991.

Duden, Jane. *The Olympics.* New York: Crestwood House, 1991.

Jarrett, William. *Timetables of Sports: The Olympics.* New York: Facts On File, 1990.

Tatlow, Peter. *The Olympics.* New York: Franklin Watts, 1988.

Index

Photo Credits
Cover: AP/Wide World Photos; back cover: AP/Wide World
Photos; p.4: AP/Wide World Photos; p.33: Jerry Cooke for Sports
Illustrated/©Time, Inc.; pp.34–35: Heinz Kluetmeier for Sports
Illustrated/©Time, Inc.; p.36: AP/Wide World Photos; p.37:
George Tiedemann for Sports Illustrated/©Time, Inc.; p.38 (top):
George Tiedemann for Sports Illustrated/©Time, Inc.; p.38
(bottom): Jerry Cooke for Sports Illustrated/©Time, Inc.; p.39:
Eric Schweikardt for Sports Illustrated/©Time, Inc.; pp.40, 41:
Heinz Kluetmeier for Sports Illustrated/©Time, Inc.; p.42 (top and
bottom): AP/Wide World Photos; p.43: John G. Zimmerman for
Sports Illustrated/©Time, Inc.; p.44 (top): AP/Wide World Photos;
p.44 (bottom): Gamma-Liaison; p.45: George Tiedemann for
Sports Illustrated/©Time, Inc.; p.46: John G. Zimmerman for
Sports Illustrated/©Time, Inc.; pp.46–47, p.48: Heinz Kluetmeier
for Sports Illustrated/©Time, Inc.

Famous Names
in
MOTORING

Christopher Pick

Other books in this series

Famous Names in Medicine
Famous Names in Crime
Famous Names in Space Exploration
Famous Names in World Exploration
Famous Names in Music
Famous Names in Science
Famous Names in Sport
Famous Names in Popular Music
Famous Names in Films
Famous Names in Seafaring
Famous Names in Aviation
Famous Names in Invention
Famous Names in Warfare
Famous Names in Football

ISBN 0 85340 766 5

© COPYRIGHT 1980 WAYLAND PUBLISHERS LTD

FIRST PUBLISHED IN 1980 BY
WAYLAND PUBLISHERS LTD
49 LANSDOWNE PLACE, HOVE
EAST SUSSEX BN3 1HF, ENGLAND

TYPESET BY COMPUTACOMP (UK) LTD, SCOTLAND
PRINTED AND BOUND IN GREAT BRITAIN
AT THE PITMAN PRESS, BATH

Contents

2201282

Gottlieb Daimler

The early days of motoring

The motor car has become so much a part of modern life that it is difficult to believe that less than one hundred years ago people still relied on horsedrawn transport. By the end of the nineteenth century, however, several engineers were working on the problem of producing a self-propelled carriage. Gottlieb Daimler devoted most of his life to solving this problem.

The main difficulty was to build an engine that would drive an ordinary carriage. Obviously the huge boilers and large coal and water supplies needed for railway locomotives were unsuitable for smaller vehicles. The first stage towards a solution of the problem was the discovery that petrol vapour mixed with air produced an explosion that could power an

engine. The next problem was to produce an engine powerful
enough to maintain a reasonable speed.

Gottlieb Daimler first worked on the problem in 1892 when
he became chief engineer for a company called Otto and
Langen. Four years later this company produced a four-stroke
engine, which was more efficient than earlier engines.

In 1882 Daimler started his own company, helped by a
brilliant designer and close friend, Wilhelm Maybach. After a
great deal of hard work they built a four-stroke engine capable
of 700 to 900 revolutions per minute, which was much faster
than anything built till then. In 1885 Daimler installed his
engine in a conventional carriage, and the following year he
finally produced a prototype purpose-built car. Daimler's first
car never went into production, however, and he had
considerable difficulty interesting people in it. However, by the
late 1890s business really began to boom, and the age of the
motor car was ushered in.

Carl Benz

Father of the motor car

Another great name in the history of motoring, Carl Benz, was also working on the problem of producing a practicable internal combustion engine.

Carl Benz had been fascinated by engines from a very early age. His first job was with a steam locomotive manufacturer, but in 1871 he left to set up his own machine shop. Business was slow, and profits were low, but Benz was determined not to give up. During the winter of 1878 he worked hard on a two-stroke internal combustion engine.

Benz's new engine was a great success and eventually proved to be the solution to his financial problems. Next he started work on a more powerful four-stroke engine. Unlike Daimler, Benz was working on the design of an entirely new vehicle — not just the engine. In 1885 his three-wheeled, two-seater car was given its first drive through the streets of Mannheim in Germany. Benz had difficulty convincing a doubtful public that this noisy, spluttering, unreliable machine had any future at all. Buyers were few and far between, even after Benz drove it 322 kilometres (200 miles) from Mannheim to a trade fair in Munich, and showed it at the 1889 Paris Exhibition.

However, in the 1890s things began to look up, and Benz became the first car manufacturer to go into regular production. In 1893 he put the Viktoria, a four-wheeled car that could travel at 19 km/h (12 mph), on sale, and it soon began to attract orders. The picture shows Benz (second right) in a Benz-Viktoria. A smaller, cheaper model, the Velo, was also popular, and by the end of the century two thousand Benz cars had been built. Carl Benz lived until 1929, well into the age of motoring he had done so much to found.

Émile Levassor

'Winner' of the first motor race

In the 1890s motoring was so new that anyone with enough talent and imagination could set up in business designing and building cars. This is just what Émile Levassor decided to do.

Levassor ran a company in Paris that manufactured woodworking machinery. He and his partner, René Panhard, were commissioned by Édouard Sarazin, Daimler's French agent, to build one of Daimler's engines. However, Sarazin died before the engine was finished. Fortunately, Levassor was able to continue work on the engine as Daimler had given Sarazin's widow the rights to build his engine in France.

Levassor's first attempts were not very practical. But in 1892 he hit on a design that really did work. It was quite crude

compared with modern vehicles, but as Levassor said, 'It's brutal — but it goes.'

Besides designing one of the first practicable cars, Levassor also entered the first motor race. It was held on public roads in 1895 from Paris to Bordeaux, and back again. First to finish, and hours ahead of his nearest rival, was Émile Levassor. He took 48 hours 48 minutes, travelling at an average speed of 24 km/h (15 mph), and drove himself all the way, as his relief driver had overslept and failed to turn up! Levassor was not declared the winner, however, as his car (shown opposite) was a two-seater, and the race authorities had stipulated that entrants' cars should seat more than two.

Another race the following year, this time from Paris to Marseilles and back, brought tragedy. Levassor's car overturned and he suffered internal injuries. Although he went back to work, he never fully recovered and died early in 1897.

Herbert Austin

Father of the baby car

Herbert Austin was once described as one of the best engineers in the world. This was a remarkable tribute, especially as it came from William Morris, Austin's great rival car manufacturer for several decades. But the 'Old Man', or 'Pa' Austin as he was known, well deserved such praise.

Austin built his first car, a three-wheeler, in his spare time in 1895. In the late 1890s he designed the first Wolseley car, and soon several different models were in production, some of which Austin raced himself.

Austin left Wolseley in 1905 to start his own motor company. By 1914 it had become one of the largest in the country, and was producing a wide range of high-powered, expensive vehicles. Some of Austin's methods were quite

unusual. For example, he was one of the first manufacturers to build both car engines and bodies in the same factory. Until then car firms built the engines, and specialist coach-builders built the bodywork.

However, Austin Motors began to lose money after the First World War. The new Austin Twenty was too expensive, and did not sell. To avoid bankruptcy Austin decided to build a baby car, which would be cheap enough for ordinary people to buy. His fellow directors were opposed to the idea, so Austin decided to go ahead on his own. He converted the billiard room in his home into a drawing-office and, helped by just one apprentice from his factory, worked day and night on the project. Within a few months the Baby Austin 7 was born, and Austin's plan proved a brilliant success. By the time production of the car stopped in 1938, over 250,000 Baby Austins had been sold.

The picture shows Herbert Austin (far right) with his racing team before the start of an event in 1923.

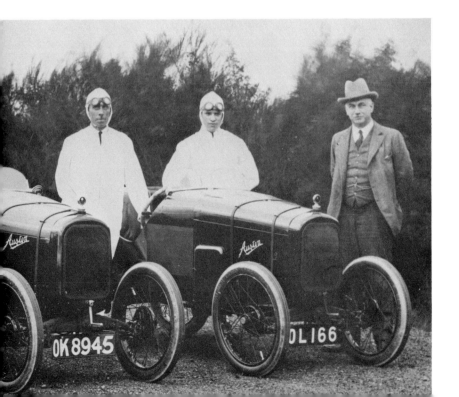

Henry Ford

Cars for the masses

In the early days of motoring cars were a luxury only the very rich could afford. Henry Ford was determined to change all that. He set out to produce a family car that ordinary people could afford to buy, and he succeeded largely by introducing a new method of car production. The picture shows Henry Ford with his first car.

Workers in the first car factories, including Ford's, built each car separately assembling the individual parts by hand. This was a time-consuming and expensive process, and only a small number of cars could be built each year.

Ford quickly realized that he would have to invent a more efficient method of producing cars. First he got his engineers to design and build machines that could manufacture parts in large quantities. Then he turned to the problem of assembling the parts, and finally came up with the idea of the moving assembly line. The car chassis was placed on the end of a belt which moved slowly through the factory. The workers sat beside the belt, and as the line passed them they had just one small job to do on the chassis. By the time the chassis reached the end of the line the car was complete.

The new system was ready by 1913, ten years after Ford had opened his first factory. Its effect was revolutionary. The number of cars built increased spectacularly, and by 1923 over two million Model T cars were being built each year. This was the famous car Ford had designed as his first popular family model. The cost of production also dropped dramatically.

Ford lived until 1947. His company, which is now run by his great-grandson, is one of the biggest car and truck manufacturers in the world.

Rolls and Royce

Nothing but the best

The world-famous partnership between Rolls and Royce began in a hotel in Manchester on 4th May 1904. How did such a meeting come about?

Henry Royce (opposite above) worked as an apprentice on the railways, and then had several other jobs before starting his own engineering business. In 1903 he bought a French car, as very few were made in Britain at that time. He was not satisfied with its performance, so he decided to build his own. The third car he built was used by Henry Edmunds, a director of Royce's company.

Charles Rolls (opposite below) had been fascinated by cars from an early age, and entered several of the first motor races. In 1902 he started a business selling cars, again mostly French ones. His aim was 'to sell the best cars in the world'. He was a friend of Henry Edmunds, and one day was invited to examine Edmunds' car — the one Royce had built. Rolls quickly recognized that this was indeed the best car he had ever seen. Rolls and Royce arranged to meet ... At first Rolls agreed to sell all the cars Royce built. Then in 1906 they formed a joint company, Rolls-Royce, and a few months later launched their first car, the famous Silver Ghost which was an instant success.

By 1908 Rolls' enthusiasm had been caught by an even newer form of transport — the aeroplane — and he retired from day-to-day work at Rolls-Royce. Two years later he was killed when his plane crashed during a flying display. In the same year Royce became seriously ill. He remained an invalid for the rest of his life, but still managed to keep in close control of the company's activities until his death in 1933. Even today the name 'Rolls-Royce' still symbolizes the 'best'.

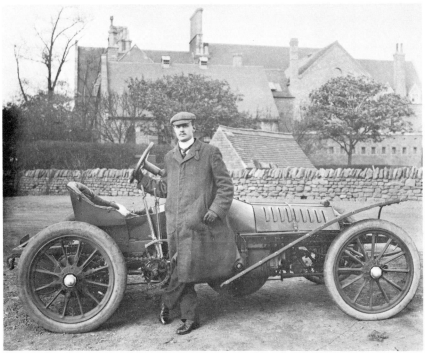

Ferdinand Porsche
Designer of the 'people's car'

Today the word Porsche has come to mean super-luxury and super-speed. But Ferdinand Porsche, an engineer of extraordinary talent, was equally at ease designing a modest family car and a racing car.

Porsche's first job was with a company that made electrical equipment. By the time he was twenty-two he had designed his first car, which was powered by electricity. Electric cars were very popular in the early twentieth century, and for a time people thought they worked better than petrol-driven cars. During the next thirty years Porsche worked for a number of different companies, including Austro-Daimler and Mercedes, producing some of their most successful cars. He also designed tractors, fire engines, and military vehicles.

In the 1930s, his most brilliant period, Porsche designed two world-famous cars. The first was the Auto Union Grand Prix car. This was the first successful rear-engined racing car ever produced.

Porsche's other major project during the 1930s was the Volkswagen car. Hitler, Chancellor of Germany, was very keen to build a small, cheap car to be sold in large numbers (the word 'Volkswagen' means 'people's car'). By 1936 Porsche had built three different prototypes, and two years later the final version was ready. However, the Volkswagen was not put on the market until several years after the end of the Second World War. It is still one of the most popular small cars in the world.

Porsche was imprisoned after the war, and was not released until 1947. He died in 1951, having lived to see his son launch the first Porsche sports car.

Ettore Bugatti

Beauty on wheels

Ettore Bugatti's childhood ambition was to be an artist, not a car designer. However, some would say he fulfilled his ambition for Bugatti cars are among the most beautiful cars ever built.

When he was seventeen, Bugatti was apprenticed to a firm of cycle manufacturers, and he immediately began to design a motor tricycle. In 1899 he entered it for the Paris–Bordeaux race, but had to retire after hitting a dog! Soon after that he began work on his first car, which he had to do at home as his employers refused to support the project. In 1909 he set up in business on his own. His first car — a small model called the Type 10 — was a great success.

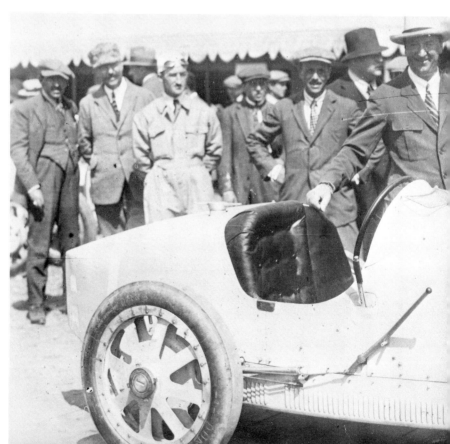

After the First World War Bugatti began to design and build larger cars. The racing models performed well throughout the 1920s and 1930s. Most successful of all was the Type 35, which dominated Grand Prix racing between 1925 and 1930, winning seven major races in the 1926 season. The road versions were eagerly sought after by connoisseurs who could afford to buy them. The picture shows Bugatti in 1924 with the famous T35 sports car.

During the early 1930s Bugatti gradually handed over much of the day-to-day running of his factory to his son, Jean, who had inherited his father's skill as a designer.

Then in August 1939 tragedy struck when Jean was killed while testing a car. Bugatti had always been an aloof man, and Jean had been his only collaborator. The factory closed, and Ettore spent the war years dreaming of cars that would never be built!

Enzo Ferrari

The 'old man' of motoring

Enzo Ferrari is probably the most experienced man in the motoring world today. His career dates back sixty years to the first race held in Europe after the First World War — the 1919 Targa Florio in which Ferrari finished ninth.

In 1920 his career took a different turn when he started to work for Alfa-Romeo. He managed their racing programme through some of its most successful years. In 1929 he left Alfa-Romeo to set up his own business, Scuderia Ferrari, which prepared both works and private Alfa-Romeos for races.

Although he never became a well-known racing driver, one victory in the 1923 Circuit of Ravenna did have important consequences. Among the spectators were the parents of the famous Italian air pilot, Francesco Baracca, who had been killed in the last months of the war. They were so impressed with Ferrari's performance that they presented him with the shield their son had mounted on his plane. Since then every Ferrari car bears the famous Prancing Horse.

After the Second World War Ferrari founded his own company to design, build and race cars under his own name. On 5th September 1948 the first Ferrari Grand Prix car made its debut in the Italian Grand Prix. Since then Ferrari and his team have had both good and bad periods. The 1950s and early 1960s were particularly successful, and World Champion Niki Lauda raced Ferrari cars to victory in the 1970s.

Ferrari — an autocratic, independent man — still runs his own company and is dedicated to maintaining the superiority of his cars. The picture shows Enzo Ferrari (the man with white hair) admiring one of his models in 1970.

Juan Manuel Fangio
Superstar of the 1950s

The legendary Juan Manuel Fangio dominated the motor racing scene throughout the 1950s. He won his first major international race in 1949 when he was thirty-eight years old — an age when many drivers are considering retirement. Two seasons later he won the World Championship for the first time — and won it again four times in the next six seasons.

Fangio was born in Balcarce, a small town in Argentina. As a young boy he was passionately interested in football. However, his second interest was cars, and as soon as he left school he got a job in a garage. He rode in his first race as a mechanic when he was seventeen, and raced his own car six years later. Success on the racetrack came slowly in the 1930s, and in 1940 and

1941 he was National Champion of Argentina.

It was not until 1949 that Fangio embarked on his first full international season. His Argentinian fans must have wondered how their hero would perform, but they need not have worried. He won his first race — and six more that season. These were the legendary years, when Fangio's skills were at their peak. He raced, and won whatever the weather or the condition of his car. Behind the wheel he was a persistent fighter, determined at all times to win — and to win fairly. Off the track he was quiet and retiring, preferring a simple lifestyle to the glamorous life of many racing drivers.

Since retiring he has built up an extremely successful motor business in his native Argentina. Whenever he attends a race anywhere in the world he is greeted by loud cheers — a reminder that the motor racing world has not forgotten this 'giant' of the track.

Tazio Nuvolari

Champion of Champions

It's the summer of 1935. Crowds are gathering at the Nür-burgring, Germany's major racetrack, for the German Grand Prix. People are talking excitedly about a German victory.

The starter's flag goes up, and the cars roar off. Almost immediately a scarlet Alfa-Romeo emerges from the fourth row to challenge the Germans. On the tenth lap it takes the lead, loses it during a pit stop, rejoins the race in sixth place and fights its way towards the front. Finally, on the last lap, it roars to victory, over two minutes ahead of its nearest rival.

This was probably Tazio Nuvolari's greatest race. He showed all the skill and determination that led many to proclaim him the world's greatest racing driver ever. With his fearless courage, spectacular style and amazing skill Nuvolari quickly became the darling of the crowds.

Nuvolari first made a name for himself competing in motor-cycling events. He remained at the top of motor-cycle racing until he finally abandoned two wheels for four in 1930. He had been racing cars long before then, however. In 1924 he crashed badly during a trial drive in an Alfa-Romeo. A week later, still bandaged and in pain, he had to be lifted on to the seat of his motorcycle for the Grand Prix des Nations, which he won in pouring rain.

During the 1930s he triumphed in Grand Prix races, cross-country racing, and long distance sports car events — in fact in almost every type of competition he entered.

Nuvolari returned to racing after the Second World War, determined to stay in the sport he loved, but fighting increasing ill health. He competed in his last race in 1950, and died three years later.

Jackie Stewart

Racing superstar

Jackie Stewart was a champion at the age of twenty-one. He had won the British, Irish, Scottish, Welsh and English Championships ... in clay pigeon shooting! However, he was disappointed when he was not selected for the British Olympic team. Gradually his interest in shooting declined, and he became increasingly absorbed in motor racing.

Jackie was no stranger to the world of motoring. His father owned a garage in Dumbarton, Scotland, and his brother, Jimmy, had raced during the 1950s. Jackie Stewart's skill on the racetrack was revealed right from the start. He took part in his first international races in 1964, and won almost every race he entered. The following year he entered his first Championship Grand Prix races. He won the Italian Grand Prix, and at the end of the season was third in the World Championship — an amazing result for a newcomer to the racetrack. In 1969 he became World Champion for the first time.

He took only fourth place in 1970, but that season saw the start of the most exciting and rewarding part of his career. Stewart had long worked with Ken Tyrrell, a former driver turned manager. Now Tyrrell started to build his own cars, and racing them Jackie Stewart won the World Championship in 1971, was placed second in 1972, and won the Championship yet again in 1973. The combination of Tyrrell/Stewart seemed unbeatable.

In 1973 Stewart retired from racing — the undisputed master of his sport, and one of its best known and most controversial figures.

Henry Segrave

Knight of speed

Friday 13th June 1930 was a sad day for the world of motoring. The entire country mourned the death of Sir Henry Segrave who was killed after his speedboat capsized on Lake Windermere. The charming, resolute Segrave had already broken the world water speed record once that day. It was typical of his single-minded determination that he should try to repeat his triumph.

Segrave was fascinated by speed from an early age. When he was only nine, he drove the family car through the lanes near his Irish country home, accompanied by an anxious chauffeur! His father knew nothing of these exploits until years after his son's death. After the First World War he became a member

of the Sunbeam racing team. He soon became determined to win the French Grand Prix, which was the most important motor racing event at that time. He achieved his ambition in 1923 finishing a full twenty minutes ahead of its nearest rival. Henry Segrave had become the first British driver ever to win a Grand Prix.

He won several other races during the next few years, but gradually turned his attention to new challenges. With virtually no financial help he decided to challenge the land speed record. In 1927 on Daytona Beach in Florida he became the first man to travel at more than 200 mph (322 km/h), beating the previous record held by Malcolm Campbell. The following year Campbell regained the record, but in 1929 Segrave triumphed once more.

By then he had his eye on the water speed record. Preparations were made, and in June 1930 he travelled to Lake Windermere. Then came that fateful Friday 13th …

Stirling Moss
Uncrowned champion

Few drivers if any can beat Stirling Moss for sheer professionalism and skill. Yet in fourteen years behind the wheel, Moss never attained the ambition of every racing driver — to become World Champion.

Moss competed in his first race when he was eighteen. That season he entered fourteen racing events — and won ten of them. At first Moss was determined to drive only British cars, which were usually no match for their European rivals. It was only when he joined the German team of Mercedes for the 1955 season that he won his first Grand Prix. From then on he was always amongst the winners, and British enthusiasts willed him to victory through every season and at every race. He came second in the World Championship in 1955, 1956, 1957, and 1958. In 1957 he endeared himself still further to the crowds by achieving the first all-British Grand Prix win (a British driver in a British car) since Segrave's triumph in 1923.

The next three seasons Moss was placed third in the World Championship, despite a bad crash in 1960. In 1962 hopes were high that he would at last win the title everyone thought he deserved. But at Easter he suffered a bad crash and was rushed to hospital, very seriously injured.

After a year of operations and convalescence Moss was well enough to give himself a test drive to discover whether he still had the razor-sharp judgement and concentration that had marked his driving. Soon afterwards he announced his retirement, with characteristic bravery preferring not to return to the track as a second-rate driver.

Jack Brabham

Triple World Champion

World Champion Driver three times; World Champion Constructor twice; the first of the modern drivers to build his own racing cars; the first to win the Championship in his own car. This is the enviable record of tough Jack Brabham.

Brabham had always been fascinated by cars, and learnt to drive when he was only twelve. At fifteen he left school to work in a garage, and after two years in the Royal Australian Air Force he opened a tiny motor repair shop. One of his first commissions was to build a new engine and chassis for midget-car racing driver, Johnny Schonberg. This gave Brabham his first experience of the racing world.

Over the next nine years Brabham gained valuable experience of really tough competitive motor sport. It was on the Australian speedways and hill-climbs that he really learnt how to handle a car, and extract every inch of performance from it.

In the mid-1950s he decided to test his skills against European competition, and came to England. Typically cautious, he left his wife and son behind in case things didn't work out — they soon joined him! After only four seasons he won his first World Championship. In 1960 he won again, taking first place in five consecutive Grands Prix.

At the end of the 1961 season Brabham formed his own company to design and build racing cars. Five years later he won the Championship yet again as well as the Constructors' Championship, and in 1967 he was runner-up to New Zealander, Denny Hulme.

Still on top form Brabham retired from racing at the end of the 1970 season, having nearly won the Championship yet again.

Malcolm Campbell

Speed King on land and water

Malcolm Campbell — nine times holder of the world land speed record, and four times holder of the world water speed record — felt the challenge of speed and adventure all his life.

He began motor racing as a hobby, and in 1910 he bought a large American car. He stayed up all night painting it blue, and decided to call it *Bluebird*. All Campbell's future cars and boats were called *Bluebird*. The First World War interrupted his racing activities, but after the war he returned to the racetrack. His greatest ambition was to become the fastest man on four wheels. In 1923 he bought the Sunbeam car in which K. L. Guinness had taken the land speed record the previous year. Renaming it *Bluebird* he took the record for the first time, reaching a speed of 235 km/h (146.16 mph) on Pendine Sands in Wales. The following year he increased his speed to 242 km/h (150.87 mph).

Meanwhile, competition from his two main rivals — Sir Henry Segrave and J. G. P. Thomas — was increasing. In 1926 Segrave took the record, followed twice by Thomas. Campbell regained it in 1927, only to be beaten again by Segrave, who became the first person to travel at 200 mph (322 km/h). Campbell regained the record at Daytona Beach in 1928, only to lose it again in 1929! By 1931 both Thomas and Segrave had died, and the field was clear for Campbell. In an even more powerful *Bluebird* he reached faster and faster speeds. Then on 3rd September 1935 he finally achieved his ambition to travel at 300 mph (483 km/h).

After this triumph Sir Malcolm announced his retirement, but only from the land speed record. He immediately turned to the water speed record which he took four times.

Alec Issigonis

'The Mini man'

Alec Issigonis is well known as the designer of the most successful small car ever built — the Mini. However, that is only one of this remarkable man's achievements.

Issigonis gained valuable practical experience in his first job, working for a small company trying to develop automatic gearchange. Issigonis' talents were not wholly absorbed by his job, and with a friend he designed a single-seater car, the Lightweight Special, which he raced in hill-climbs and sprints. In 1936 he joined Morris Motors, where he spent the rest of his working life, except for four years during the 1950s. Soon he was put in charge of developing a completely new car, which finally appeared in 1948 as the Morris Minor. The compact, economical Morris Minor was an immediate success and

continued in production until 1970. The millionth model rolled off the assembly line in 1961 — the first British car ever made in such numbers.

Issigonis' next triumph came in 1959. After the 1956 Suez crisis which threatened Britain's petrol supplies, Issigonis was asked to design a car which did not use much petrol. He came up with a revolutionary design. The layout of the engine was completely new. Although the car was so small it allowed maximum space for passengers and luggage. The interior of the car was rather spartan, but the low price of only £496 more than made up for that. Since then many different versions of the Mini have been produced, and by June 1979 over four-and-a-half million had been sold. The Mini has also won countless rallies and races.

Sir Alec retired in 1971, but he is still full of new ideas and continues to work closely with car designers and engineers. The picture shows Sir Alec Issigonis at his retirement party with the first Mini and other landmarks in his career.

Colin Chapman

Luxury on wheels

Colin Chapman is undoubtedly one of Britain's greatest motoring success stories. He has not only been responsible for some of the world's most successful racing cars and run his own racing team, but has also designed and built some of the most luxurious high-performance sports cars — the cars of everyone's dreams. He also achieved one of his earliest ambitions — to be a millionaire by the time he was forty.

In 1947, while he was still a student, Chapman designed, built and raced his first car. This was a modified version of the tiny Austin Seven. Improved versions followed quickly, and by 1951 he was getting so many orders that he formed his own company — Lotus Engineering. Chapman was always full of new ideas, and established his reputation as a designer during the 1950s. Gradually Lotus cars began to win races.

The early 1960s brought Lotus their first triumphs in Grand Prix racing. In 1960 the Lotus 18 won thirteen of the nineteen major events for which it was entered. In 1962 the Mark 25 startled the racing world with its new aerodynamic design, which was eventually adopted by most other designers. Since then Lotus have maintained their success, winning the Constructors' Championship seven times. Lotus drivers have won the World Championship six times.

Chapman's success on the racetrack has been accompanied by equal success on the road. The design of the current Lotus models — the Elite, the Eclat and the Esprit — owes much to the experience Chapman gained on the racetrack.

The picture shows Colin Chapman (right) with Jackie Stewart and Graham Hill.

Roger Clark
Racing round the clock

Rallying is one of the most demanding forms of motor sport. Rally-drivers must be really skilful — as well as driving fast they have to negotiate extremely difficult terrain often in poor weather, maintaining total concentration for hours at a time. Roger Clark, one of Britain's finest rally-drivers, has proved himself master of all these skills.

During his rally-driving career he has crossed the Canadian prairies, driven flat out over the Khyber Pass, raced through the Australian desert, scaled the high peaks of South America, and struggled through snow and ice in the forests of Scotland.

Roger Clark could hardly reach the pedals when he drove a car for the first time — he was only eight! At school he disliked academic work, preferring to concentrate on practical subjects, and on 'winning things'. After leaving school, he became involved in motor sport, and drove in his first rally in about 1960.

Clark quickly became convinced that rallying was the sport for him, and he spent most of his weekends competing in rallies all over the country. He had his first victory in February 1961, and immediately afterwards took part in his first international rally, the Circuit of Ireland. In 1964 he drove his first Ford, a Cortina GT, and two years later became a popular and respected member of the Ford works team.

Since then Clark has won nearly all the major rallies at least once. Among the highlights of his career are no less than six victories in the International Scottish Rally and, most outstanding of all, wins in the big RAC Rally of Great Britain in 1972 and 1976.

Tom Wheatcroft
The man with a dream

In the 1930s Donington Park, near Derby, was one of Britain's major motor racing circuits. Among the spectators there one day in 1936, watching his first race, was a fourteen-year-old apprentice plasterer named Tom Wheatcroft.

Thirty-five years later, in 1971, Donington Park gained a new owner — that same Tom Wheatcroft who had become one of Britain's most successful builders. Two years later 'Wheatie', as much of the racing world knows him, opened the Donington Collection, which is one of the largest collections of racing cars in the world. In 1978 the circuit itself was re-opened for racing.

The late 1930s were Donington's greatest years, and Tom

Wheatcroft never missed a race, sometimes sleeping in a little tent so that he could be up early to watch the morning practice.

Gradually he became more and more involved in the sport, and started to back drivers and build up a collection of cars. The first drivers he supported — Derek Bell and Roger Williamson — were both unknowns who needed a helping hand. They got one and more with characteristic Wheatcroft generosity. Then one day in 1973 Roger Williamson was killed when the tyre tread came off his car. Wheatcroft was sickened by the tragedy, and has never backed a driver since.

The Wheatcroft Collection started almost by chance. Wheatcroft bought a Ferrari 125 to drive himself, then another and another. Soon he had a dozen cars, then twenty-five, then forty ... Today the Collection numbers nearly a hundred cars. Tom Wheatcroft's plans for Donington do not end there. His next aim is to bring the British Grand Prix back to its former illustrious home.

John & Edward Scott-Montagu
The motoring Montagus

The present Lord Montagu and his father have perhaps done as much as anyone else for motorists in Britain.

John Scott-Montagu studied history at Oxford University. When he left the university in 1888, he got a job with the London and South Western Railway, and became a skilled locomotive driver.

In the late 1890s motoring was just becoming popular in Britain, and John Scott-Montagu was one of the first people to buy a car. Some of his relations considered him a 'dangerous revolutionary' for doing so! For the rest of his life he did all he could to popularize the new form of transport. He was the first Member of Parliament to arrive at the House of Commons in a car. He also took the Prince of Wales (later King Edward II) on his first car drive (shown opposite below). His car was the first British car to race on the continent. Not content with all this, he also founded a motoring magazine, *Car Illustrated*, persuaded Parliament to raise the speed limit from 12.5 to 20 mph, and even, fifty years ahead of his time, argued powerfully in favour of motorways.

Edward Scott-Montagu, third Lord Montagu, has continued his father's work. He is most famous for building up the National Motor Museum at Beaulieu. There were only six cars on display when the Museum opened in 1952, but it now houses over 300 exhibits. Cars from the collection often take part in vintage rallies, and television and film producers from all over the world often use them for their programmes. Lord Montagu has also founded an important motoring publication, *The Veteran and Vintage Magazine*, and often takes part in House of Lords' debates on transport topics.

Glossary

Chassis the frame, wheels, engine and other mechanical parts of a car to which the body is attached.

Circuit a motor racing track.

Cross-country races motor races run on ordinary roads through many different types of countryside.

Grand Prix races motor races held each year to determine the World Champion Driver. *See* World Championship.

Hill-climbs races against the clock held over difficult terrain in hilly and mountainous areas.

Marque term used to designate all the different models produced by one manufacturer.

Midget car racing the sport of racing midget, or under-sized, cars which emerged in the 1940s and quickly became popular.

Pit an area at the side of a motor-racing track where drivers can refuel, and if necessary service, their cars.

RAC Royal Automobile Club, the controlling body of motor sport in Britain.

Rallying a type of motoring competition over public and closed roads in which cars (adapted from models produced for public use) compete over a course made up of a number of stages with control points along the route.

Season the months of the year during which motoring racing takes place, usually February to October.

Speedway racing on specially built tracks, which are often oval.

World Championship the most important motor racing competition which is held every year. There are 15 qualifying Grand Prix races, and the points of each driver's best 9 races are totalled to determine the World Champion.

Reading List

Cars by Christopher Pick (Galley Press, 1979)
The Encyclopaedia of the Motorcar edited by Phil Drackett
(Octopus, 1979)
Great Racing Drivers by Doug Nye (Hamlyn, 1977)
The Horseless Carriage by Lord Montagu (Wayland, 1974)
Motor Racing edited by Geoffrey Nicholson (Macdonald,
1973)
Motor Sport, a Pictorial History by Raymond Flower (Collins,
1975)
Racing Cars and Bikes by Robert Royston (Macdonald
Educational, 1977)
Rally! by John Davenport (Hamlyn, 1976)
Veteran and Vintage Cars by David Burgess Wise (Hamlyn,
1970)
The Young Engineer's Book of Supercars by Jonathan Rutland
(Usborne, 1978)

Picture Acknowledgements

BBC Hulton Picture Library 28–9; John Topham Picture Library 22–3,
34, 40; Keystone Press Agency 21; Mary Evans Picture Library 8;
National Motor Museum 4, 9, 15 (both), 16, 18–19, 25, 30, 39, 45
(both); Sport and General Press Agency Ltd. 27, 33. The publisher
would like to thank the following for their help in providing pictures:
Austin Morris Ltd. 10–11, 36–7; Ford Motor Co. 13; Geoffrey
Goddard 42–3; Mercedes-Benz 5.

Index